Rants and Raves of an Indie eBook Publisher!

Achieving Success with Digital Books

by: James M. Lowrance © 2012

I0472927

TABLE OF CONTENTS:

INTRODUCTION

Within the chapters that follow, I will offer tips to other indie/independent authors who are considering publishing their eBooks with sellers such as the Amazon KDP and NOOK (Barnes & Noble) publishing platforms. I will additionally include some information regarding my personal experiences writing for content websites (sites that publish articles in exchange for ad-revenue shares), in consideration of the fact that many indie publishers begin their writing experience with these type venues before advancing onward to eBook publishing.

While I may at times have straightforward things to say about advantages or disadvantages involved in publishing and selling through these types of venues, I do not resort to degrading language toward those I have had less-than-positive experiences with. I will also be frank regarding sales or publishing issues I have experienced, as an independent author but since I do share much of this information from personal perspective, there will be a few inevitable rants and raves added-in from time to time.

My best publishing experiences have been with the Amazon Company, both their Kindle Direct Publishing (eBooks) and their CreateSpace (paperbacks) divisions.

This doesn't mean that I don't have good things to say about other publishing platforms because I certainly do but the outcomes I experienced do not reflect what every independent publisher will experience with same venues or platforms. Many factors are involved in publishing success, including the genres one plans to cover (types and subjects of eBooks being published) and how one plans to promote them. At the same time, I feel there are things we can learn from fellow-publisher experiences.

If you're a publisher, especially of the indie type, I believe you will find my shared experiences to be interesting (some more than others but with each hopefully conveying a "lesson learned"). It is my hope that readers of this eBook, will glean a few helpful nuggets of information that will lend positively toward their own ongoing publishing experiences, including advice regarding cautions that should sometimes be taken when proceeding with the different types of venues that are available for developing authors.

-Jim Lowrance

CHAPTER ONE

Publish Your eBook Free on Amazon KDP

In this chapter-installment, I will start with a "rave" -- my own report of positive experience with the Amazon eBook publishing platform. I hope to convey the fact of how the platform offers ease-of-use, plus how it gives indie eBook publishers the advantage of having their works placed before a massive worldwide consumer audience and amazingly, it's completely free! I would like to also add at the front of this chapter, that I am not associated with the Amazon company, in any other fashion, other than being a very pleased user of their publishing/selling tools. Keep in mind that there are other free eBook publishing platforms available, including Barnes and Noble's "Pubit" program, which also offers ease-of-use for indie publishers and most authors will place at least some of their titles with multiple reputable sellers.

I felt that offering a rundown of the steps needed to publish eBook works, will help those who are new to this venue or who have not yet published eBooks on their own (those who have previously used fee-based publishers only), a general idea of how a publishing platform works, by using Amazon KDP as an example.

In simple terms, an author actually only needs a completed eBook (formatted for reading by consumers) and also an attractive cover-image if possible, to place their work live on an eBook seller website, that offers a publishing platform.

I personally sell 100s of units between my eBook and book titles at Amazon each month, most of these being through KDP, which I began using in early year-2008 (it has never stopped growing and the numbers may someday reach into the 1,000s monthly). I love the fact that the platform also allows me to go into my eBook files and make revisions, such as corrections or adding more content to them, at any time following their original publication. I want to generally go through the steps for publishing eBooks on Amazon, via their free service, which was formerly called the "Digital Text Platform" and now called "Kindle Direct Publishing".

Obviously, before one can publish a written-work, it needs to contain interesting, enjoyable or helpful content and it needs to be formatted, so that it is of good quality and readability. Spacing paragraphs, adding chapter-headings and including an introduction and table of contents, can all be important to adding quality and consumer-appeal to an eBook. Having a cover-image for it can also add appeal to it, especially one that is professional-looking in appearance.

Or that is at least relatively close to a level of professionalism. If you do not have a cover for your eBook, Amazon KDP will provide a generic one (a "placeholder image" that looks quite good) but a personalized one is of course better when possible.

Independent publishers ("indies") have a great opportunity to have their works sold through Amazon via this eBook publishing platform and the mega visitor traffic their sites experience worldwide, is highly promoting for eBooks. You can register with KDP to publish eBooks, via this link: https://kdp.amazon.com/self-publishing/signin.

Once you are a registered member and you have a completed eBook you are wanting to publish with them, click on the "Add a New Title" button that appears near the top-page of your bookshelf (the publishing area of your account) and then complete the following steps I have numbered from "1. to 14." shown below (it seems like a lot to complete but it is much easier than it appears and it becomes easier with each use of the tools they provide).

1. Click on the yellow "Add New Title" button near the top of your KDP Bookshelf page and then click in the "New Title 1" bar it will take you to on a new page (near the top again) and type in your eBook title.

2. Skip all the prompts below the title bar (unless the title is part of a book series, in which case you fill these in as directed) and then skip-down to the "Description" form and paste or type your eBook description-details into it.

3. Click on the "Add Contributors" button and when the spaces pop-up, add your name by typing it into the first and last name spaces and click the "Author" option in the drop-down menu (or other contributor ID option that applies) which further identifies you (there's also an optional "publisher" space and you can add your name again into that or skip it if you like).

4. The "Language" bar that indicates the language your eBook is written-in, should already say "English" in it, so leave it alone if that's the case or choose the correct language option in the drop-down menu.

5. In the "Publication Date" space, click on the miniature calendar beside it and click on "Today's Date" or choose/click another date within the month if you like.

6. Under "publishing Rights" click the little circle next to "this is not a public domain work", if this is the case (the "public domain" choice is for non-copyrighted works).

7. Click on the "Add Categories" button and choose up-to 2 of them from the drop-down menu (you may also have to click-on sub-categories that appear out beside the main ones, to better ID your eBook genres/categories). Also be sure to add your "keywords" in the bar provided for them (up to 7 are allowed and should be descriptive toward your eBook's subject-matter). The keywords are important in that they help your titles to be categorized better and to be more readily found by people doing search engine and Amazon site browsing.

8. Click the "Browse for Image" button and choose your eBook image from your computer (I usually use images that are between 1200 and 1285 pixels on each side) and after clicking the "upload" button, wait for it to say "upload successful" (the image may look unclear in the little window on the publishing platform page but will look clear on the Amazon website). The image tool will re-size your image as needed but if it is too far off from being a compatible size to be modified, it may warn you, that your image needs re-sized a bit and resubmitted (there are a number of free image resizing sites online for getting this done if needed).

9. Click the little circle that says "Enable Digital Rights Management" (unless you opt not to have it).

This protection against people copying/pasting your work) -- it is optional. Your automatic copyright protects you from outright theft of your written work, regardless of the option you choose on this particular prompt.

10. Click the "Browse for Book" button and load your word.doc or PDF file, until it says "Download Successful". You can then click the prompt to review your eBook if you like, which will appear in a reader on the page that looks similar to how it appears on Kindle devices (I love being able to review my submitted eBooks before finalizing publication of them).

11. Under the "Verify Publishing Territories" heading, click the little circle that chooses "Worldwide Rights - All Territories" (unless there are countries you wish to exclude via the other options that are shown within these prompts).

12. Under the heading "Please Select Royalty Option", choose the "70%" option, if your eBook is priced at between 2.99 and 9.99 (if it is higher or lower than this range, you'll have to choose the 35% option). These are the amounts of commissions/royalties you will make on unit sales of your eBooks and the amounts are calculated for you (to the exact dollars and cents), once you enter your retail price.

13. Under "List Price", you'll see a bar for typing-in your eBook's retail price, at the top of the squared-in area and after filling it in, you then click the little boxes beside each of the other countries that are listed and this will automatically set the price for them as well, comparable to your listed-price first typed-in for the U.S. Amazon website (calculations are based on the value of U.S. currency, as compared to that of the other countries).

14. The last little square on the page that appears just above the "Save and Publish" button, needs to be clicked because it simply confirms your rights to publish the eBook and afterward, you either click the "Save and Publish" button or the "Save for Later" button (use the latter if you want to recheck things or make changes before the final publishing).

NOTE: the little square prompt beside the "Kindle Book Lending" heading is already pre-clicked and is why we skipped this one (it cannot be un-clicked). NOTE: Amazon also offers a program called "KDP Select", in which borrowed eBooks also earn commissions for publishers. It is an optional program, which will be covered further in chapters that follow.

Another good thing about the KDP publishing platform, is the fact that if you overlook completing a step, it will tell you.

It does this by highlighting the incomplete areas in red and it will not allow you to publish your eBook, until you go back and complete them. Just like anything else, the process becomes simpler each time you use it and once you've published several eBooks, it becomes easy for you.

In adding a final note for this chapter, I will mention that if you use a publisher such as "Smashwords", which submits your eBook titles to multiple sellers including Amazon, this process is completed for you. The choice to use such a publisher is largely based on the amount of control an indie desires to have regarding the immediate monitoring of sales reports and exclusive self-promotion of published titles. I personally made the decision to publish my own eBook titles to each seller myself but as the saying goes "to each his own", some indies may prefer the option of having everything completed for them, regarding publishing and sales tracking.

CHAPTER TWO

The BooksOnBoard eBook Publishing Platform

During the final months of year 2011, I received an email from the BooksOnBoard bookseller website, inviting me to submit my eBook titles to them as an indie publisher. They stated in the invitation email that they were only inviting a small number of independents to participate in the new program and that I was one of them. I actually felt privileged to be one of the indies who were invited and I began submitting my titles immediately. I submitted a total of 54 titles to their new publishing platform and within a couple of weeks, they placed 21 of these live on their website. They looked very nice on the site, in-fact, as nice as the book/eBook ads that the main booksellers were displaying. I also liked the browsing/search features of their site and I understood why they were the largest independent book selling company, existing online.

After my first 21 submitted eBooks were placed live, they had to take them back down temporarily, in order to edit something regarding the descriptions of them, having to do with the imprints, which needed to show the author as self-publishing them.

They informed me about this change, by email and while I awaited the republishing of them, I received a notice from Amazon as well, regarding their new "KPD Select" -- an eBook borrowing program, for Amazon consumers participating in it. For eBook publishers who enter their titles in this program exclusively for 90 day increments, a commission is paid on titles that are borrowed by consumers. I decided to place nearly two-thirds of my own titles into KPD Select and before BooksOnBoard could republish mine, following their needed changes to the imprints on them, I emailed them, asking that they please not place any of them live again until I further notified them. This would give me time to determine which of my titles would still be available to other eBook sellers and not be exclusive to Amazon Select.

I eventually did notify them but their reply by email stated that many indies who originally submitted eBooks to them, did the same as I did, by afterward asking that theirs be removed, so that they could include them in participation with KPD Select. They stated in the email, that they had obtained the services of a secondary company to operate the publishing platform and that the adding, followed by removal of many titles originally submitted by indie publishers, had proven to be expensive.

They were suspending the publishing platform for independents and would only be doing business with established publishing companies, until further notice.

I appreciated their notification to me, describing their reasons and while I sincerely felt regret for having participated in causing this problem for them, I also knew that my participation in the new Amazon program was a necessary move for me. At the same time this occurred, I was having ongoing problems with several other booksellers, while my Amazon experience was very solid and this continues to be the case. In-short, I have never been treated better as an indie publisher but this does not mean that I don't see great merit in some of the other booksellers out there, who may very well begin to create more success for indies over time. As they do, I will have the same commitment and appreciation for them, in keeping my titles on their websites.

I still believe that I will always have a certain percent of my titles enlisted in KPD Select, for as long as it continues to be available (hopefully permanently) but this will still leave lots of them available for republishing with the other booksellers who remain solid with sales reporting and eBook/book search capabilities on their websites.

I do hope that BooksOnBoard reopens the eBook publishing platform because they appear to be a solid company with great growth-potential for independents. Should they again invite more indie publishers to participate in a publishing platform again, in the future, I will be try to be one of the first in line, to resubmit my non-exclusive titles to them, if I am accepted. They are a quality bookseller and I would welcome the opportunity.

I added the preceding information in this chapter, to demonstrate the fact that competition between booksellers, can sometimes result in these types of scenarios taking place and in fact companies have been known to literally dissolve as a result of fierce competition that causes them massive loss in market shares. I personally hope to see several major booksellers to continue their availability to indie publishers because this helps us to avoid having all of our eggs in one basket so-to-speak and helps us to experience the ongoing expansion of our titles that we are seeking.

CHAPTER THREE

Mean-Spirited Spam Book and eBook Reviews

As an author of eBooks and paperbacks, I occasionally see book reviews appear on my works, at seller websites like Amazon and Barnes and Noble. I will now add somewhat of a "rant" regarding negative reviews in this chapter.

Spam Reviews

Most reviews I see posted for my published titles, are at least moderately favorable toward my authored works and some are very positive but ever-so-often, I will see one appear that is flat-out mean-spirited or those that actually amount to spam reviews. I have only actually flagged one of these negative types in all of the time I have been publishing on bookseller's websites (since 2008) and the reason I did-so in that case was due to the review-poster literally slamming a book I have available on the subject of Chronic Fatigue Syndrome and Fibromyalgia, in order for them to also recommend another author's book that they stated was "better than all other books available on the subject put together".

Amazingly, the bookseller whose site the spam review appears on, for some reason did not detect the review as containing spam and yet by even the strictest definition, that is exactly what it amounted to.

Booksellers Should Screen Mean-Spirited Reviews

The review poster actually included the wording to the effect that my eBook on the subject was "a rip-off" and they actually titled the review to the effect of "don't waste your money". I was amazed that the bookseller allowed the review to be posted and I am monitoring it to see if they will remove it, after my having flagged it. I will also mention that the reviewer claimed that the eBook was "too short "and yet it contains 12 chapters and over 9,000 words, at a price of only $2.99. I have fellow-publisher friends who I exchange book reviews with on-occasion and one of them has already posted a favorable review for the same eBook, after I provided them a free copy for adding their own review, in order to help offset the negative one (I recommend this method when unfairly negative reviews appear on titles deserving better reader-comments). A better review that was added behind the spam one.

It mentions the fact that one of the chapters contained in my eBook title, was awarded an "editor's choice award" in 2009, when it was previously published by a reputable content website. This will help to offset the attack-review should the bookseller for some reason, not remove it (at the time of this writing, it has remained for several months).

Illegitimate and Unethical Reasons for Negative Book Reviews

Why do people write extremely unkind reviews that obviously are not merited by a published work? In some cases, these are actually posted by real readers who are simply venting their frustrations toward books they have read that did not meet a standard of perfection they were seeking or that did not solve a problem for them as well as they had hoped. I know for a fact that other authors experience the spam and overly-negative book review scenario because I have been told this by them, firsthand.

In some cases, reviewers may resent the fact that an author was able to publish a book on a subject that they failed to accomplish written works on their selves.

They may have their own authored work available and they feel they can direct more attention toward it by degrading work published by other authors, on the same genre or subject. Some readers of this article-post might actually ask at this point, if I really believe this type of scenario takes place and I would respond by saying that **I certainly do**. In some cases, these type reviews are posted by fans of other writers or by friends of them, which would be far more acceptable, if it is a positive review for their own titles, rather than unfair negative reviews for titles by authors that they feel are competing with them.

Another reason I know for a fact that overly-negative and spam reviews result from the type scenarios I describe above, is due to my having been informed about this by writers-groups who enter into arrangements for exchanging positive reviews with each other. I have so-far only exchanged reviews with two authors, on less than a dozen of my approximate 70 published titles because I prefer to see them posted by readers, who are simply consumers but I do have these fellow authors on standby, to review any titles I see attack-reviews appear on, so that they can offset them by posting a counter-review with more positive language included in it.

I always tell them to rate the book honestly and to not include any biased favoritism in it (this would not be doing the author a favor).

Red Flags

The fact is that booksellers will not publish works that are obviously poor-quality or that are lacking enough content in them. Of course there are titles published by authors that are not deserving of praise or that do deserve a degree of criticism however, when reviews are overboard in the negative direction or include attack language or literally tell consumers to not buy a title, this should raise red flags with booksellers. As previously mentioned, these type reviews can simply be posted by consumers who are venting frustrations because a book was not as life-changing as they had hoped it to be or they may be posted by authors or friends/fans of authors who are hoping to curve any competition they feel competing titles may present them.

I will also mention that the same seller who allowed the overboard review for one of my titles, that I describe above, also recently allowed another highly-negative review on another eBook I have published on their site and in this case I honestly believe the reviewer did not purchase the title.

I believe this due to my having the title unpublished for a period of time and I had not sold a copy of it on the seller's site for a number of months. The review appeared in February of this year (2012) and yet the bookseller did not sell a single copy of the eBook during that month or for five months previous. This makes the review highly suspicious.

Of course a book-title might simply be legitimately bad but if this is the case, why would a bookseller allow such a title to be published in the first place or to continue being offered for sell? No, in most cases, overly-negative or attacking reviews that sometimes contain spam language, are simply not legitimate and authors should be prepared to report these or to offset the negative effects of them by soliciting additional reviews from ethical readers of their titles.

CHAPTER FOUR

Amazon's KDP Select: A Sales Boom for Me!

During the December month of year-2011, I decided to place a significant number of my eBook titles into "Amazon KDP Select" - a promotional commission-paying, eBook borrowing program that requires exclusivity of titles you place into it (for 90 days at a time). I had less than half of the month of December left when I placed mine there and I saw about a dozen borrows of various titles right off the bat! Now that January has almost swung-past (at the time of this writing) my number of borrows has already reached "21" in number. I feel however, that part of the promotional power of the program is the notation on your titles on Amazon, showing them to be available for borrow by KDP Select members, which in-itself promotes both borrows and sales of them. It adds just that bit more of interest for consumers to check into the titles further when they see this notation added to them.
The reason I believe the program promotes both sales and borrows is due to the fact that my sales through Amazon in-general have spiked, since placing them there.

I will admit that I'm proud of how my sales and promotion for my titles has evolved on Amazon.

They have simply done very well by me and I'm as pleased as can be, to be a part of this vastly-growing company, as an indie publisher. Some publishers, both indie and companies, might see sales numbers like mine (in the 100s per month) and find them to be low in-comparison to their novels and romance titles, that have massive outside promotions for them however, my title-sales (mine being mostly health disorder subjects) are seeing steady growth at Amazon and for an indie with limited promotional power, I feel my numbers are quite good.

The increase I'm seeing through KDP Select is significant and I'm anxious to see what coming months/years will reveal sales-wise. As I have stated in past online articles, my love of writing is not based on profits from sales, although I certainly enjoy that aspect but it is also my love for sharing information I believe will be helpful or inspirational to others. So when my numbers go up, much of my enjoyment and pleasure from writing, is knowing I have reached more readers.

Are there both pros and cons to placing eBook titles into a program like KDP Select? It actually kind-of depends on how you look at it but the short answer is "yes, there are both pros and cons". I've already described the pro aspects, from my perspective/experience.

Now I'll mention a couple of the drawbacks. "Exclusivity" places all your eggs into one basket so-to-speak, if you enter every title you have into this type program. A publisher might instead place only their select or prime titles into exclusivity and leave others on different seller-sites. The other drawback is that sellers you might remove titles from, to place into this type program, might feel a bit slighted for you having done so.

When I made the decision to place most of mine into the program, I removed them from the BooksOnBoard seller, among others however, they had already taken my titles down from their site to make a change to the imprints on them as mentioned in a previous chapter, so I caught them at the point before they reapplied them to their website. I actually told them to hold-off on republishing them and I added that I hoped I was not "burning a bridge with them". Once I knew which of my titles I would not be placing into KDP Select, I wrote BooksOnBoard again and listed the titles I wanted to publish with them. They eventually wrote me back, stating that they were discontinuing the program for indie eBook publishers, at least for a period of time, due to many of them switching many of their titles to KDP Select exclusivity, as I did.

Sellers should be open to publishers protecting their interests, in this type situation because they would do exactly the same thing for their own businesses if a similar opportunity had arisen for them. I can absolutely be solid and faithful to a seller who does me right and who I'm doing right and I will openly praise them but "business is business" and sometimes difficult decisions have to be made. When I make changes that aren't always in the interest of someone else I might be in arrangement with, I always do-so respectfully and always without burning bridges if at-all possible. Beyond this, I'm not sure what else a person can do, when they are protecting the interests of their life's work (I spent literally 1,000s of hours over an 8 year period writing my works and they are very important to me).

There's always that possibility that a program like KDP Select will fizzle-out over time and my belief is that this is why they only require 90 day exclusive increments on publisher's eBook titles but right now, the program looks like it might be a growing and ongoing success for sales and promotions of eBooks -- and for me, it has literally started with a boom.

CHAPTER FIVE

Is it a Good Thing to Write for Content Websites?

I mentioned in my introduction, that I would be relating some experiences I have had with publishing articles on content websites, which is something I did for several years before I entered the eBook and paperback book publishing venues. In this chapter, I will be relating my past experience writing for a particular site that is one of the more reputable ones in their field. Let me also immediately say at the start of this chapter, that I personally have no reason to believe the company has committed anything unethical or dishonest. I can say that they are extremely business-protective-oriented (a logical attitude to the proper extent).

Writers who contract with content websites like the one I will be referring to, are literally the "life-blood of their companies" and who have brought them to their past and present growth-status. This could not have happened for them without quality content from authors and these sites would not exist today without the vast flow of articles being submitted to them.

The Removal of 50,000 Articles

From July 2009 to February 2010, I authored 117 articles that were carried live by this website and after they removed approximately 50,000 articles, at the start of year-2012 (yes, that's right -- *fifty thousand*), in order to improve their website-ratings, this still left 91 of my articles on the site (they removed 26 of mine). They informed their writers, about the article removal, via their account pages, rather than by email (at least I never received an emailed notice) and within their explanation, they stated clearly that the removal of the content was not a reflection of the quality of the writers but was rather due to them implementing much stricter editorial guidelines. They also stated that in some cases of articles being carried by them, it was their selection process "getting it wrong" -- the implication being that their editors should not have approved these articles in the first place. Some websites, have also cited the new enforced website guidelines called "PANDA" and "Farmer" (required updates), that brings rating penalties against websites that fail to adhere to them, as a major reason for their decline in success and readership growth.

Why I Resigned as a Writer for the Content Website

In 2010, when I resigned as a writer from the website, it was due to my ongoing problems with editing changes/requests. This had nothing to do with their asking me to make changes to articles I submitted (I always did-so immediately upon request) but it rather had to do with liberties one editor in-particular, was taking, by making major changes to some of my articles, without rather asking me to make them myself (administration seemingly did not recognize the seriousness of the problem, involving a writer's copyright). My experience in no way, reflects the practices of the site in general and the lack of attention to the problem, may have been due to miscommunications that occurred within the site-administration. I felt a need to mention this because I also dealt with a number of great people there, in spite of my negative experience in regard to the particular editor I refer to.

I will admit that I would not have agreed to some of the requests made by this editor, had I been asked to make them myself but it was blatantly wrong for them to make some of these changes, without my prior agreement to allow them. Small obviously-needed changes by an editor were certainly fine with me, in giving them liberty to make them. This included overlooked misspellings.

It also showed small changes to improper structure or punctuation mistakes) but changing the meaning of the content itself was unacceptable to me. If I refused any requested changes required beyond these simple types, they could have then simply denied publication of the article in question. I would have then published the rejected-article on another website or on my personal blog.

To be more specific regarding this issue; I began submitting articles under the "religion" category -- specifically ones for the "Christian" section of the website (I believe this specific category has since been eliminated from their sites), several of which still appear live there and a number of these were on the subject of Bible prophecy. The editor, who has since been promoted to a senior editor position, was apparently a bit biased toward psychic phenomenon and in places within articles, where I used the word "prophecy", she replaced it with the word "predictions". The biblical word "prophecy" is considered absolute by Christians while the psychic word "prediction" implies "a percent of probability or failure" for a foreseen event to transpire. I explained this to the editor and let her know that I could not allow the word-changes to remain and so I changed them back to the proper words and she afterward, dropped that particular requirement.

The same editor also began to re-write sentences and sometimes entire paragraphs within my Christian topic articles, so that they had more of a psychic or spiritism/mysticism flavor to them (for lack of better terms). She also began to argue with me regarding the interpretation of certain Bible passages I was writing on, at which point I complained to the site administration. To make it clear, let me mention that the interpretational remarks I made within articles, were those of general agreement within a large percent of the fundamental Christian community and I know this to be a fact, due to my being in Christian ministry and evangelism for nearly 20 years (1983 to 2001) and graduating theological studies with Liberty University in 1996. The debate this editor engaged in with me, actually became a bit bizarre because once I would explain why I took the position I did with a biblical doctrine, she would bring up another aspect to argue with me about (I joined the Christian topic to write and **not to debate biblical interpretations**).

I Received a Reprimand for My Complaint

The site administration who became aware of my complaint, immediately defended the editor in question. They praised her highly and stated that they felt it was improper for me to have made a complaint.

This, despite my email being fileded in a business-like manner and my disagreement containing **no disrespectful language** toward the editor. They made me feel as if it was improper for me to have contacted them regarding the issue and yet my disagreement addressed directly to the editor was not taken seriously by her and the issues were not resolved. I knew her disagreements with my articles, which were actually based on "meaning" rather than "editing" aspects, would have continued to be written by me, under the heading that I wanted to submit many more articles under (my goal was to eventually have1,000 articles live on their site -- with many new health titles also planned). At this point, I took my issue to their writers-forum and posted about it there because I knew I was leaving/resigning as a writer and I felt the issue was important for the sake of future writers and that proper attention was not given to it, in spite of the obvious infringing nature of it. I was also reprimanded for posting as a member on the private forum about the issue but my resorting to the posting, was due to failure for resolution via email communications.

Other Issues at the Content Website

Another issue that I felt was causing some difficulty at the content website, was their announcing frequent "writing challenges".

This would be contests such as "30 articles in 30 days" (plus many other variations of push for increased content), meaning if writers completed this many articles, within a given time-frame, they would be listed among the achievers on the website, via a recognition page. This seemed like a push to increase the numbers of content for the site, quickly and yet they wanted articles to meet a strict guideline for quality (an obvious conflict between quality and the number of content-pieces being coerced from writers). It was likely during these times, that editors became overwhelmed and had no choice but to approve articles coming to them for editing, in huge numbers. These may very well include some of the articles they have recently removed from the site in huge numbers.

When I began writing for them over two years ago, there were times I saw "PV (3 months)" at over 61,000 and I saw my revenue per month at over $100.00 at times and fluctuating between $50.00 and $75.00 for a number of months. As of this January month of 2012 my "PV (3 months)" is 7,554 and my revenue split has been running at an average of about $10.00 for the past 3 or 4 months. Profit has never been my only reason for writing as previously mentioned.

For the first two years I wrote articles online in-general, I wanted nothing in return for them but readership. When it comes to a website that enforces very strict editing guidelines, writers are certainly worth a split of the profit they are making for these content, revenue-sharing venues. It's possible that their cutting back of 50,000 articles that were under-par, will help them to gain back a higher rating and market share (only time will tell). **I sincerely <u>do not</u> wish them ill** and I actually hope the downturn recovers for them.

I wrote to them a few times over the past several months, to see if I would receive a response but they would not reply to me, in spite of my sending messages to several people within their administration. I tested this further, by sending request to be reinstated as a writer but still no response from anyone. The last time I wrote them (January 2012), I asked that my remaining 91 articles be removed from their site -- still no response from them of any kind.

What Does the Future Hold for Content Sites?

Another website I wrote-for, during a short time period, in year-2011, actually did the same thing.

In attempt to recover from a downturn in site popularity they removed 1,000s of slightly less quality articles (I removed my own remaining ones at that point). In the case of this content property, the cutback of articles did not improve the site's status according to a recent article in "The Freelancer Today" online magazine and they have discontinued writing availability to non-professionals and are now only working with a very few select writers. All other freelance writers were given notice of discontinued revenue share and writing access, as of December 15, 2012. The same article that reported the failure of this other content website, which also reported on a major downturn in popularity for the "Life123" content website, posed the question as to whether this same future might be in store for other highly successful content websites such as "Demand Studios", which is reported by some sources, to now be the largest freelance, revenue-sharing content website on the market today.

I would ask this same question regarding the content site my articles still appear on. -- Will they follow the same downward trend or will they recover? Current writers for them will simply have to wait and see. There is question posed by this chapter's title, regarding whether or not content websites are a good thing to write for.

I would answer by saying that under the right circumstances and conditions, which likely varies between each writer and each website, they are potentially a very good venue write for. I do suggest that writers are careful to read the terms and contracts offered by them and to make sure these allow for them to remove their articles if necessary, free-and-clear of any retained rights to the content by the website, so that they can move them to better publishing venues. (More on the content websites subject in CHAPTER SEVEN)

CHAPTER SIX

My Recent Bizarre Experience on a Publishers Help Board

With this being an eBook in which I am relating personal experiences, I wanted to add a chapter in regard to an experience I had recently at a forum for publishers of eBooks, provided by a major bookseller (not associated with an Amazon company). Please note that this article is not intended to imply that the forum I refer to, is not a helpful place of information exchange for publishers because I believe it is and let it also be understood that bad experiences on forums can potentially happen on any of them regardless of their purpose and quality.

Why I'm relating this Experience

I have several reasons for wanting to relate this experience, the main one being the fact that forum-posting is a form of online publishing. I also want this article-post to offer some warning regarding forum involvement in general. Forums and message boards can be wonderful things when they are moderated correctly but those that have inadequate moderation (very sparse, imbalanced or near non-existent) can become more of a hindrance than a help for users.

I do not place the Publishers Help Board I describe in this chapter, into the negative category because I believe it to be a **largely helpful forum**. I will add however, that the experience I had there (described below), though likely rare, demonstrates the fact that one should proceed with forum activity, with reasonable caution. One importance in the need for caution, comes from the fact that negative exchanges are indexed online, indefinitely and can be viewed by readers who see these types of posts that are connected to the authors, who also have eBook titles for sale (many use their titles in their forum signatures and profile bylines).

Let me also mention before I begin relating the experience I had at the forum, that this is only one of dozens of times I have either experienced similar scenarios at forums or have seen them occur to other members of them. In at least one case, I actually saw a forum taken offline as a result of negative postings (attack and harassment posts), with the majority of its posts being taken out of index by search engines as well. In the past, I served as a moderator at several forums and my own combined posts at these approached approximately 5,000 in number. I became experienced enough at spotting negative behaviors at them, to know when it was evolving into harassment or attacks between members.

A Worse Case Scenario for Non-Moderated Forms

On one other forum I will mention, at a very popular content website, the "Religion & Spirituality" forum, evolved into a place of continual religious bigotry that was as vile as it can become, with every possible foul word, including the "f-word" being directed at members. I not only discontinued any involvement in the site-forum but I removed approximately 275 articles I had on the correlating content website, due to their administration not removing the offensive posts and being absent in regard to moderation (I cover this experience in another of my book/ebook titles). Even non-moderated forums require intervention by their providers if things get out of hand on them.

My Publisher Help Board Incident

Now on to my forum experience (Please again understand that this does not reflect the standard of the forum in-general and I'm relating this experience due to it being associated with a "publishing" platform.):

Approximately 15 months ago at the time of this writing, I joined this Help Board.

This was to communicate with fellow-publishers. My total number of posts over the 15 months was "127" (105 of these were replies), many of these were on the subject of formatting and other eBook-publishing related topics. Admittedly, of the 22 thread-topics I started personally, many were in regard to "sales reporting issues "that were occurring with the associated eBook publishing platform (sales being delayed in being applied to publisher's reports) and some of these threads were follow-up ones, in-which I would report a problem being fixed. Some of my posts, all of which averaged less than 8 per month, would not have continued on the subject, except for the fact that the problem with sales reporting continued. The site administration actually informed publishers that the problem was occurring, both by emails to us and by occasional forum updates. In spite of this fact, there were times it took them several weeks to become informed about the issue as it would recur (a fact confirmed by them thanking publishers on the forum, for making them aware of it).

The Bizarre Attack Posts

At one point, one of the forum members launched an attack toward me, complaining that I was posting too-frequently

They felt I was posting too frequently regarding the ongoing problem with sales reports and related issues (they are still fixing related problems, even as I write this chapter) and I was taken-back by this fact because first of all, it was for the benefit of all publishers that the problem continued to be pointed out by members, for resolution to occur. I was literally advised by a man with this site's Business office, a year previous to this, whom I spoke to by phone that their administration needed "frequent and straightforward communication" or they might not respond or investigate complaints, due to them being overwhelmed with emails. He literally stated to me that "you have to shout at them to get their attention" (a verbatim quote). After about 15 months of their eBook publishing platform being in business, they are now starting to put significant fixes on the issues publishers have been experiencing/reporting since its launch in late September, 2010 (I have 24 ebook-titles that continue to be listed there) but this has required diligence on our part.

Why Attack When you can Ignore?

The forum member who attacked me for my part on the forum, in attempting to get the needed attention on the sales reporting issues, should have simply avoided those threads.

However, since another member at the forum PM'd me (personal message), stating that they-too had been attacked by this individual, I knew his complaint regarding my posts **was not legitimate**. Whatever his true problems are they are not actually caused by the posts of forum members (there is something deeper involved). Coincidentally, this member would post regarding the fact that he had eBooks published on the associated platform but he refused to list the names of any of his titles. This allowed him to post attack-threads without readers of them connecting his forum behavior to his published titles, which as a result, could potentially affect consumer perception of his character in general (something he was obviously avoiding).

The problem with this scenario, is the fact that people can potentially pose as authors by joining a forum, but who in-reality have not published any titles. In some cases, they join forums in order to market services of some type -- which is something this member was also doing (he was making an eBook formatting service available and using the forum to advertise it). The best solution to this possibility in my opinion, is for the forum-administration to require new members to list at least one of their titles on their forum signatures, to confirm their status as legitimate authors.

Strangely, this member posted in a thread, claiming I had posted on the subject in-question (problems with sales tracking/reporting), "4,398,743 times", which of course was meant for sarcasm. I posted a thread to correct this claim and included no attack language within it whatsoever but I did address it underline to this member and an Administrator/Moderator censored (removed) my corrective post (it was likely flagged by the other member who could apparently dish-out harassment but who could not withstand correction for it). His posts however, which did include attack language and harassment within them have been allowed to remain on the forum (due to my not flagging any of his). My feeling is that the moderator could not investigate the problem as well as it should have been, possibly due to time constraints. The option to "ignore" the posts on my part was hindered by the fact they were directed at me and were not ones I saw between other members that I could have easily bypassed.

I actually sent this member who started the negative exchange, an apology PM and this is the response I received back from him, shown in italics below (I PM'd him a total of "4" times - - 2 of them attempts at apologies):

His Reply:

*"You have some serious issues if you're still crying over something some random stranger said to you on the internet weeks ago (.
Let me explain it a different way - STOP MESSAGING ME. I have no desire to hear from you, I don't care about anything you have to say, be it an apology or whatever. Geezus I feel bad for any chick that ever tried to break up with you because if it's this hard for me to get rid of you, being a complete stranger, my guess is you stalked ex's for years.
G O A W A Y"*

(Note: This reply I received following my apology-attempt, was an attempt to reverse the scenario -- to claim I was pursuing an argument and that I was the one on the attack or who has "serious issues". Also: While I relate this experience, I do not hold a grudge against this man but sincerely wish him recovery from whatever his problem may actually be.)

When Legitimate Business Threads are Hijacked

This is the attitude of the individual who was not moderated on the forum.

Shown in in italics above and as a corrective point, it <u>was not</u> a "random something" he directed at me but rather a series of posts he addressed me with, in several threads. This is the reason I no longer participate in posting on that forum (respectfully). I felt that business threads, literally having to do with publisher's livelihoods, should not have been hijacked and degraded by this individual, who may or may not actually be an author.

In reflecting back to what the associated website employee advised me by phone (to be persistent), he also told me that a common complaint of publishers was "no reply to emails" and that they needed to put attention-getting headers on them and to send them repeatedly if-needed, to solicit a response. This is basically what some of us were doing through the provided venue of the "Publishers Help Board", as an alternative to overwhelming them with emails.

My Concluding Advice Regarding Publisher Forums

If a person who joins a forum, finds that they can't resist the urge to attack other members, my suggestion would be to read other's posts as it helps but **not to post**.

Also, when someone who is a posting member reacts with disagreement to a thread that is offensive to them or one that is posted for the purpose of attack or harassment, they should bypass those threads and not read them (very simple). It's the same principle one uses when they watch television but they are not interested in what they see on certain channels -- just change to a different one!

If you cannot help but see something on a publicly-displayed TV station that literally goes out-of-bounds and should rather be restricted to certain age-groups or that should not be on the air at-all due to bigotry or other issues, simply contact the cable company, the network or satellite provider, just as you would contact the moderator or administration of a website that provides a forum. It may or may not help but we do our best to keep these venues from degrading and to remain helpful for those they are intended for. Believe it or not, there are actually social forums designed for attack posts, "contests of wits" or that are sexually explicit, etc... If a forum is not of these types but is designed to help people but begins to degrade due to lack of moderation and legitimate members do not attempt to do something about it, this can contribute to a negative direction for publisher-forums in general.

Online forums have genuine potential that can be both positive and negative but much of this depends on proper administration to moderate/remove potentially negative posts and threads.

CHAPTER SEVEN

Content Farms: Authors Beware!

Content websites glean articles from writers/authors who are looking to publish their works online. There are literally 1,000s of these type of sites that are now often referred-to as "content farms". Some sites might see this term as being derogatory however, in many cases, this term describes these types of writing venues correctly because they are in-essence planting seeds of advertisement toward potential content contributors, they then grow a base of articles from the resulting response and they can then harvest the advertising money from it. If they fairly split profits with content contributors who write for them, this can be a good thing, in addition to providing authors with readership exposure.

Contracts that Give Websites Permanent Ownership of Articles

This chapter's title is meant to get the attention of writers/authors who are considering writing for such venues. **They can be genuinely good opportunities** in some cases however, some sites offer contracts to writers that are overly-biased toward them.

Some contracts for example, state that the content contributed to them by contracted author/members, becomes their property perpetually (forever) and it also cannot be removed at any point by the contributor, including for the purpose of compilation into eBooks. In some cases, this type term is also stated with exclusivity attached to it, meaning it not only belongs to the site in-question, eternally but the author cannot at any time publish any content submitted to them, any place else online, in-print or in digital form of any type. This would include placing the content on other websites or into books and eBooks as previously mentioned. Even if such a term is not exclusive to them, it may still grant a website in-question the right to permanently market your content, regardless of what you may also being doing with it at any given point in time.

Some of these strict-policy websites also block authors from being able to go into their contributed articles and make changes to them, once they have passed their editorial standards and are approved for going live. This of course also includes the inability to remove a piece at any point afterward as previously mentioned.

What adds insult-to-injury, is the fact that the extended publishing of an author's content at these type content websites, may not pay any additional commissions/earnings to the author. The ad-sharing revenue of the site (or whatever type of compensation is offered), may be restricted to that which is earned on their main website but not from any outside sources they may also market the content to. The site can then harvest the extra income without splitting a percent of it with authors.

My Negative Experience with a "How To" Property

To give an example of a website I experienced this very scenario with, I will refer to a "How To" type property (website specializing in articles on how to do certain things). They were splitting ad revenue with authors for the first couple of years they were in business but at one point, they simply decided to discontinue the revenue sharing. Their reasoning offered, was that they were going to a different type of format for their website however, they continued to have paid-advertisers and were still a profit website. They had gleaned literally 10s of 1,000s of articles from authors before making this change to a nonprofit sharing site. They were the type site that also blocked the ability for authors to change or remove articles when this major change occurred.

I was unable to remove my content from their site, so I wrote them, threatening legal mediation. To my surprise, this worked, without any further action required on my part and they removed my content from their website.

Another amazing thing regarding this incident, was the fact that the site had taken author's content and they began to advertise it as little eBooks guides, on a major bookseller's website. None of the authors were told about this and we simply came across our articles, offered in eBook form, inadvertently via online search. I mentioned the fact of my having found my content for sale as eBooks, to the website administration when I had my content removed and they eventually also stopped advertising it on the bookseller site. Their explanation for having started this added selling venture, was to say that they entered into an arrangement with an outside company who was doing the eBook marketing. Regardless, authors were seriously taken advantage of in the case of this "How To" property-website.

Some Content Websites are good to Authors

Is there dishonesty and unfairness in the content website industry?

I believe this chapter demonstrates that this is indeed the case however, this does not take away from the fact that there are honest ones out there that treat authors fairly and honestly. I believe it also demonstrates the importance in carefully considering the terms included in content contributor contracts before entering into them with these type of writer-opportunity websites.

CHAPTER EIGHT

Why I Write Short Subject Health eBooks/Books

My shorter-subject books/eBooks, are often in the approximate 6,000 word range, with some being over 12,000 words and I still consider them short subjects. I price the vast majority of them at $2.99, in order for them to be in Amazon's higher commission bracket of 70% versus 35% but they can be as high as $9.99 to meet that requirement. A range of $2.99 to $9.99 is the price range for the 70% commission category as mentioned in a previous chapter.

My First eBooks

When I first began publishing eBooks, it was at the prompting of a thyroid disease website I contributed a dozen or so articles to in year-2005, who asked if I would supply them an eBook to offer their readers. This website was in the UK and I provided them an eBook on the subject of hypothyroidism (underactive thyroid gland). When the site administrator received it, he asked if I could shorten it a bit.

His experience with the site and its correlating forum, brought him to realize that readers wanting some education regarding a disease they are suffering, prefer eBooks that come straight to the point regarding the facts they are seeking (I actually thought the eBook was already short in length before the editing request). He added that many readers prefer not having to trudge through info-sources on specific subjects that are overly-descriptive, that veer-off into tangents or that include lots of references to other info-sources the writer might have learned their information from.

The Type of Book: A Deciding Factor for Page-Length

While my next statement might be met with disagreement by readers, who are also fellow-publishers of eBooks/books that are on similar subjects I write on, in many cases, the types of lengthy info I describe above is added, simply to extend the number of pages, which is a selling-point in a book's description. Do understand that I am not referring to books with several sections because in this case, each section can cover a different subject. I have a number of books that are lengthy and contain multiple sections (my lengthiest is 420 pages that are 8.5 X 11.5 in size) but this-too is understood in the book-description.

I also want to make it clear that books for "pleasure reading" are **a very different story**. In this case, readers love those with lots of length to them. This would include novels and works of both fiction and non-fiction that tell intriguing or interesting stories or that provide interesting information for the enjoyment of the reader.

Online Search and General Educational Resources (Books & eBooks)

When it comes to readers who have been newly diagnosed with a disease or health disorder of some type for example, and the typical scenario is involved in-which their doctor simply does not have the time to provide them anything more than a very scant education regarding it, many will seek further information from other sources. Most will begin to search online, hopefully at reputable medical sources but in the old days before the popularity of the internet, they would seek their info by talking to other people suffering their same disease or they would search their local library for books on the subject. Certainly many people still do this and some do-so, in addition to conducting an online search.

The problem that sometimes arises, is that each online source one might search, may cover a subject scantly.

However, the major points and still not include the detail one is seeking that provides them a better, **general education** regarding a disease they are suffering. I'm still not referring to information that is so intense that it would be equal to that needed to earn a master's degree on the subject but thorough-enough and with the needed-detail, to satisfy their need to be as educated as a layperson (non-professional) can be. I will admit that this can be a difficult balance to strike for an author of disease/health subjects and it's unlikely that any of us have ever done so to absolute perfection. We have to proceed with the details of a written-work, as our hearts lead us, including how we feel about book/eBook length, based on our experiences with the reading public and what we have learned from other authors and content source administrators (i.e. websites and forums).

Experience Equals Writing Methods

I formerly served as a forum moderator for patient support of those with thyroid diseases, at several websites (including being topic editor for one of the connected websites) and a common complaint I saw and one that was actually directed at my own posts on occasion, was that they were too-lengthy.

I tend to be a very detailed person and fellow forum members would at times tell me that they preferred not to see long blocks of information or ones that included too-much detail or that were loaded-down with too much medically technical language. I actually had doctors who wrote me, asking how I treated my patients who had certain types of diseases or symptoms and I had to let them know that I am not a medical professional or a doctor of any type but rather a well-studied layperson.

The combination of all of these experiences helped me to arrive at decisions regarding the length of disease-subject eBooks I wrote from that point forward and the style of information they contain. I have since written many short subject eBooks, plus, for those readers who do prefer lengthier books that cover all related subjects within a main-heading, I have also written a number of those type. So-far, my short subjects ones, on a book-by-book basis, have had a higher response by about a 10 to 1 ratio. Strangely enough, I occasionally have a reader post a review under one of my eBook titles, saying it was "too-short" and so here we have the diversity of types of readers that sometimes manifests. I suppose in these cases, the famous saying attributed to Abraham Lincoln can be referred-to: *"You can please some of the people all of the time and all of the people some of the time but you can't please all of the people all of the time."*

Apparently the advice I received from the UK website administrator back in about year-2005, has largely proven to be the case, at least in regard to the genre of disease subjects I have written about but desired book-lengths vary greatly to consumers, depending on the genre or subject-matter that is covered by them.

It is my hope that the advice I have offered within this chapter and within the preceding ones, including the occasional "rants and raves", have provided some nuggets of sound information, for consideration by the readers of them.

(END)

www.ingramcontent.com/pod-product-compliance
Lightning Source LLC
Chambersburg PA
CBHW071636170526
45166CB00003B/1343